T0129636

THE PRACTICAL STRATEGIES SERIES
IN GIFTED EDUCATION

series editors
FRANCES A. KARNES & KRISTEN R. STEPHENS

Teaching Gifted Students in the Inclusive Classroom

Tracy L. Riley, Ph.D.

Routledge
Taylor & Francis Group

NEW YORK AND LONDON

First published 2011 by Prufrock Press Inc.

Published 2021 by Routledge
605 Third Avenue, New York, NY 10017
2 Park Square, Milton Park, Abingdon, Oxon OX14 4RN

Routledge is an imprint of the Taylor & Francis Group, an informa business

ISBN 13: 978-1-59363-704-0 (pbk)

Contents

The Practical Strategies Series in Gifted Education offers teachers, counselors, administrators, parents, and other interested parties up-to-date instructional techniques and information on a variety of issues pertinent to the field of gifted education. Each guide addresses a focused topic and is written by an individual with authority on the issue. Several guides have been published. Among the titles are:

- *Acceleration Strategies for Teaching Gifted Learners*
- *Curriculum Compacting: An Easy Start to Differentiating for High-Potential Students*
- *Enrichment Opportunities for Gifted Learners*
- *Independent Study for Gifted Learners*
- *Motivating Gifted Learners*
- *Questioning Strategies for Teaching the Gifted*
- *Social & Emotional Teaching Strategies*
- *Using Media & Technology With Gifted Students*

For a current listing of available guides within the series, please contact Prufrock Press at 800-998-2208 or visit http://www.prufrock.com.

When students enter today's classrooms, they bring their different cultures, abilities, religions, families, difficulties, socioeconomic status levels, experiences, backgrounds, ways of learning, expectations, motivations . . . the list goes on. The changing demographics of families and communities also mean that students bring a need for belonging and acceptance. Educational reform, by way of inclusion, has changed schooling in attempts to reflect, acknowledge, accommodate, and celebrate these individual differences. How can teachers provide learning opportunities matched to individual needs while still maintaining a sense of community in inclusive classrooms? This is the challenge faced today by many teachers working in schools marked by ever-increasing diversity.

Gifted and talented students are part of this diverse group of learners. These students often learn at a quicker rate; understand and comprehend at deeper levels; and have knowledge, skills, and interests that are markedly different from their same-age peers. Appropriate learning for gifted and talented students is adjusted in pace, depth, and breadth through differentiated curricula that are both enriched and accelerated. This is often accomplished through segregated programs, both within and outside of school; however, the reality is that these students continue to spend the majority of their education in general classroom settings. The regular classroom has always been, and will remain, the primary educational context in which most gifted and talented students are taught. Teachers are confronted with the demands of providing appropriate learning opportunities matched to their students' exceptional abilities, but without threatening students' sense of belonging to a community of learners.

Acknowledging gifted and talented students and accepting their place in inclusive classrooms "necessitates changes or modifications to the content, processes, and products of learning in all classrooms, for all gifted and talented students, with all teachers, all of the time" (Riley, 2009, p. 634). Teachers of gifted and talented students make these changes through carefully planned and evaluated, qualitatively differentiated learning opportunities. Qualitatively differentiated learning is marked by different kinds of learning experiences, not more of the same. Modifications made to learning are noticeable by dissimilarity, not similarity. In other words, differentiation for gifted and talented students may be altogether different from that which works for other students. There is no single right way to differentiate, just as there is no single way of being or feeling gifted and talented.

This book provides teachers with practical strategies for identifying and meeting the abilities and needs of gifted and talented students through differentiation in general classroom settings. It begins by examining the common methods of determining individual differences in learning. From there, the key principles of differentiation are explained. These theoretical underpinnings are translated into practice through classroom-based and schoolwide strategies. Practical resources for teachers are also provided.

Getting Started: Understanding Gifted and Talented Students

Although there are many definitions of gifted and talented students, and list upon list of their common characteristics, it is important to remember that no two students are exactly alike. Each gifted and talented student has unique cognitive and affective strengths, abilities, qualities, and interests. In order to understand each individual student, it is important that teachers use ongoing formal and informal assessment, including the many methods of identification (Riley, 2009).

If a student has been identified by his or her school or by another agency as gifted and talented, teachers can start with information from any formal screening and identification processes. This might include observational checklists, parent nomination, formal and informal tests, peer nomination, and self-inventories. Formal identification of giftedness and talent then becomes a means to an end, not an end in itself. Many schools document this information in the student's cumulative records, or records may be held by parents or by a gifted education specialist. Looking beyond the gifted label and analyzing why and how a student meets a set of criteria will allow teachers to better understand each individual's strengths and weaknesses.

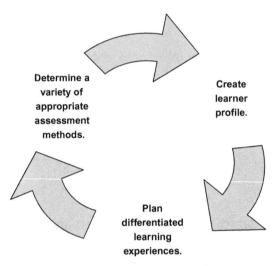

Figure 1. Cycle of differentiation.

Ongoing assessment is commonplace in all classrooms, and the information gathered through assessment must also inform teaching and learning. Teachers need to study the results and use these to trigger differentiation (Braggett, 1994; Tomlinson, 1999). To do this, teachers take the following steps:

- Determine appropriate assessment methods and use a variety of these.
- Use the data gathered through assessment to create a learner profile.
- Use the learner profile to plan differentiated learning experiences.

Within each learning experience, further assessment is undertaken, the profile is reshaped, and new learning experiences are designed. There is a cyclical pattern of assessment informing differentiation and differentiation informing assessment, as Figure 1 shows.

There are three types of assessment that will help teachers understand their gifted and talented students:

- *Preassessment* determines ability and interest prior to teaching.
- *Formative assessment* regularly monitors learning, and informs teaching and self-regulated learning through feedback.
- *Summative assessment* summarizes learning up to a point or over a period of time (e.g., at the end of a term or unit of study).

One of the most highly recommended and easily implemented practices in gifted education is the use of preassessment. Preassessment can be used to determine student readiness; preferred ways of learning; and attitudes toward, interest in, and questions about a particular topic or subject. Basically, teachers assess students before teaching even begins by using the typical assessment tools planned for the end of a learning experience. Tests, checklists, quizzes, class discussions, journal entries, products, performances, and portfolios can be used for informing differentiation as well as for showing continuous progress and mastery. In addition to traditional measures, teachers can use these preassessment tools:

- *Five Most Difficult First*: Teachers ask the five trickiest questions or toughest problems at the beginning, not the end, of an assessment, and if a student can answer these, then differentiation is warranted.
- *Mind Mapping*: Students use key words to visually represent their knowledge, skills, and interests.
- *K-W Chart*: Using a T-chart, students can detail what they already know and what they want to know.
- *Entrance/Exit Cards*: Students respond to one or two questions either at the start of a lesson (entrance) to determine understanding or at the end of a lesson (exit) to inform future teaching and learning.
- *Yes! No! Maybe So? Cards*: Students make cards to flash at the teacher in response to introductory ques-

tions (Brighton, 2005; Roberts & Roberts, 2009; Winebrenner, 2001).

Most of these tools will provide an indication of readiness, but how does a teacher determine students' preferred ways of learning, interests, and attitudes? Tomlinson (1999) suggested that teachers give all students an opportunity to share these by graphing their perceived strengths and weaknesses; writing autobiographies of themselves as learners; or answering questions about their school experiences, best and worst subjects, or preferences for learning. Setting learning goals, designing personal shields, contributing to a class book, and going on a people hunt are ideas Riley (2009) described. Just talking with students, watching them on the playground or sports field, and observing their interactions and conversations with others will provide powerful anecdotal evidence. Parents can also provide useful information about their children's passions, what turns them on and off with regard to learning, their experiences, and so on.

Finally, there are formal interest and learning style inventories, like Kettle, Renzulli, and Rizza's (n.d.) *My Way . . . An Expression Style Instrument* or Renzulli's (1996) *Interest-A-Lyzer*. Rogers (2002), in *Re-Forming Gifted Education*, and Winebrenner (2001), in *Teaching Gifted Students in the Regular Classroom*, also included interest inventories in the supplementary materials. Douglas (2004) suggested *Psychology for Kids: 40 Fun Experiments That Help You Learn About Yourself* by Kincher (1995) for informally determining personality characteristics. A gifted and talented specialist should also be able to recommend other, more formal inventories.

The information amassed will be rich and diverse, so how do teachers make sense of it all? Rogers (2002) recommended the development of a learner profile that includes educational data such as grades or tests scores, interests, preferences, and learning styles. This information could be compiled electronically or in a cumulative folder that could be shared from teacher to teacher, with the students, and with their parents.

McIntyre and Mery (2004) took this suggestion a step further, stating that an Individual Education Plan (IEP) should be developed with a primary focus on the general classroom—not on supplementary, part-time programs. Such a process mirrors that used with children with special educational needs, and is comprehensive and inclusive of teachers, specialists, parents, and, if appropriate, students, with regular evaluative checks on progress and effectiveness.

Preassessment forms the basis for differentiation in general classrooms. But what is differentiation? As George (1997) explained, it is the "process of assessing individual needs and responding with appropriate learning experiences" (p. 10). When differentiating instruction, "teachers begin where students are" (Tomlinson, 1999, p. 2), by "changing the pace, level, or kind of instruction . . . in response to individual learners' needs, styles, or interests" (Heacox, 2002, p. 5). For all students, the goal of differentiation is to create lifelong, autonomous learners (Betts, 2004), ensuring passion for learning, growth, and development. Working out the individual differences students bring to classrooms is pivotal in providing differentiated, appropriate educational experiences matched to learning needs, interests, abilities, qualities, and preferences.

Differentiation: The Basics

As stated in the Introduction, differentiation means that adjustments are made to content, processes, and products to better suit individual students' needs. *Content* refers to what students are taught and learn; *processes* refer to how students are taught and learn; and *products* refer to the outcomes or ways in which students demonstrate what they have learned. As a result of changes to content, processes, and products of learning, the environment must also be modified. In a responsive classroom environment, the responsibility for making these adaptations lies with the teacher, the individual students, and the entire community of learners (Tomlinson, 2004).

For gifted and talented learners, it is important that the changes be *qualitative* rather than quantitative: not simply more of the same, but carefully planned opportunities matched to individual needs and capitalizing upon strengths and interests. Differentiation should also underlie experiences that are both enriched and accelerated. Enrichment refers to the horizontal broadening of curricular aims and objectives, while acceleration is a vertical movement through those objectives. Acceleration, then, refers to introducing curriculum early or quickening the pace at which it is delivered. Whether a student's learning is accelerated or enriched, it will be most effective if changes are also made to the content, processes, and products.

Table 1 is a compilation of the key principles of qualitative differentiation for gifted and talented students. These can be applied across the curriculum, for all age groups, and in response to individuals. They also can be applied to strategies in the regular classroom, as discussed in the next section of this book.

Table 1
Principles of Qualitative Differentiation

Content should be:	Processes should be:	Products should be:
• Abstract; centered around broad-based themes, issues, and problems	• Independent and self-directed, yet balanced with recognition of the value of group dynamics	• Created with the aim of developing self-under-standing, specifically in relation to giftedness
• Integrated, making multidisciplinary connections	• Inclusive of a service component or an oppor-tunity to share outcomes for the good of others (e.g., the community or family)	• Facilitated by mentors as well as teachers
• In-depth and with breadth		• Geared toward considering real problems, chal-lenging existing ideas, and creating new ones
• Self-selected based upon student interests and strengths	• Stimulating of higher levels of thinking (analysis, synthesis, and evaluation)	• Developed using new and real techniques, mate-rials, and ideas
• Planned, comprehensive, related, and mutually reinforcing	• Creative, with the chance to identify problems and solve them	• Evaluated appropriately and with specific criteria, including self-evaluation
• Culturally inclusive, appropriate, and relevant	• Accelerated in both pace and exposure	• Self-selected
• Advanced in both complexity and sophistication	• Designed to integrate basic skills and higher level skills	• Wide in variety
• Gender-balanced and inclusive		• Designed for an appropriate audience
• Enriched with variety, novelty, and diversity	• Open-ended, using discovery or problem-based learning strategies	• Made to transform ideas and shift students from consuming information to producing knowledge
• Embedded within methods of inquiry, emulating the work of professionals	• Reflective of the real world, mirroring the roles, skills, and expertise of practitioners	
• Inclusive of moral, ethical, and personal dimen-sions	• Designed to develop research skills; time man-agement, organizational, and planning abilities; decision-making processes; and personal goal-setting	
• Explored through the study of the lives of gifted people	• Metacognitive, allowing students to reflect upon their own ways of thinking and learning	

Note. Adapted from "Qualitative Differentiation for Gifted and Talents Students" by T. Riley, in D. McAlpine and R. Moltzen (Eds.), *Gifted and Talented: New Zealand Perspectives* (2nd ed., p. 355), 2004, Palmerston North, New Zealand: Massey University. Copyright © 2004 Massey University. Adapted with permission.

The art of differentiation is shifting the principles outlined previously into practice. This can be achieved through a number of strategies, and it is the combination of these that is most effective. A singular strategy, used in isolation, should be avoided, as should a one-size-fits-all approach. These strategies can be implemented by individual teachers in their classrooms, but they are enhanced by using schoolwide organizational strategies. Therefore, the modifications may be to lessons, assignments, or scheduling (McGrail, 2005), within a classroom or across a school. This section outlines individual practices and is followed by a discussion of schoolwide strategies.

In Your Own Classroom

The most highly recommended practice was developed by Reis, Burns, and Renzulli (1992) and is called curriculum compacting. Basically, a teacher begins by predetermining the learning objectives, then uses an appropriate method of pre-assessing students' mastery of those objectives, and concludes, importantly, with replacement strategies for previously mastered material. This approach avoids any needless repetition of learning by documenting what students already know and can do. The careful documentation of mastery means that the elimination of quizzes, homework, drills and practice, worksheets, and other tasks related to already-mastered content, processes, or products is well justified. Reis et al. (1992) created The Compactor, an easy-to-use document that provides spaces for teachers to:

- *Name it* by providing a brief description of the material to be covered and evidence to support why compacting may be needed.
- *Prove it* by describing what material is to be eliminated and evidence of its mastery.
- *Change it* by providing an explanation of the enrichment and/or acceleration activities to extend the regular curriculum.

Curriculum compacting allows students to move ahead through acceleration or to stretch outwards through enrichment. Replacement strategies are not designed for remediation. As Winebrenner (2001) advised, "Never use the time students buy back from strength areas to remediate learning weaknesses. Always allow students to capitalize on their strengths through activities that extend their exceptional abilities" (p. 33). Renzulli and Reis (n.d.) referred to replacement activities as "student buy-backs" and declared that this can be one of the most exciting elements of teaching.

Teachers should begin exploring curriculum compacting with a small group of students, rather than as a whole-class approach. Students for whom compacting might work well are quick or early finishers, high academic performers, or even daydreamers. It is easy to identify students who are advanced beyond their peers, who may appear bored, who show creativity, who ask many questions, who assist their peers, or who bring in extra reading materials. Teachers then need to select a content area in which documenting mastery and providing replacement activities would be easily achieved and supported by ample resources. Experimenting with pretesting methods, determining cutoff scores or levels for mastery, compacting by topic (rather than by time), determining documentation methods, and exploring alternative activities require teachers who are willing to experiment, field-test, reflect, and change.

If teachers begin with curriculum compacting, the next logical step is to employ the remaining strategies highlighted in this section of the book. The replacement strategies teachers can use include independent or small-group study, learning centers, learning agreements, tiered instruction, flexible grouping, and meaningful menus. These strategies complement one another and are most effective when used in combination rather than in isolation.

Independent or Small-Group Study

Independent or small-group study is another often-cited strategy for giving students opportunities for enrichment and acceleration. Riley (2009) referred to this approach as "spin outs," because when facilitated by teachers, independent or small-group studies can provide students opportunities for moving "out and away from the basics to those areas representative of their individual strengths and interests" (p. 643). These studies can be teacher-directed, involve a required product, or be student-driven (Heacox, 2002), but in all cases they should be connected to the regular curriculum. However, it is important that in the implementation of this strategy, a balance is sought that allows students to pursue their passions without being confined to a limited set of curricular aims and objectives (Riley, 2009).

Ideally, small-group or independent study should facilitate an in-depth investigation of student-selected and authentic content, processes, and products. As Riley (2009) stated, "Although they can be structured in different ways, the most important element is that of student choice, particularly in the selection of the topic to be investigated and the final outcome, or product" (p. 643). Siegle (1998) stated that for many gifted students, having greater freedom in making decisions about their learning is the most positive element of differentiated learning. This requires collaboration between students and their teachers in setting goals, making decisions, and agreeing on working conditions and expectations (Winebrenner, 2001).

Johnsen and Goree (2005) summarized independent or small-group study as being:

- self-directed, or in groups, team-directed;
- mirroring processes of a professional practitioner or authentic to a discipline;
- facilitated and monitored by a teacher, mentor, or older student or adult; and
- focused on lifelike content, processes, and products connected with—but not tied to—the regular curriculum.

As this list of defining characteristics indicates, the role of the teacher is critical, but also must shift from traditional teacher to that of facilitator. Johnsen (2005) compared this type of teacher to a coach, one who can guide students through the stages of planning, teaching, reflecting, and applying. In the planning stages, the coach helps the students clarify goals, work through any worries or concerns, and devise strategic plans and methods, including data sourcing, collection, and analysis. As these plans are put into place, the coach moves into teaching, observing, and assisting the students as needed. Once the plans have all been enacted, the coach guides the students through reflections of what was undertaken and what was achieved. Finally, the coach works alongside the students to determine the applicability of the new skills and knowledge in future situations.

The steps a coach or facilitator takes in the implementation of independent or small-group study include:

1. *Topic Selection*: A student may already have many ideas, and as Smutny, Walker, and Meckstroth (1997) reminded, it may be helpful for the teacher to interview the child. Student interest inventories and assessment results may also provide some direction for topics.

2. *Topic Browsing*: Heacox (2002) and Winebrenner (2001) recommended giving students a chance to browse a topic,

especially if their initial idea is too broad. Browsing a topic means that students read, talk with others, search the Internet, and familiarize themselves with a big idea in order to decide on a smaller subtopic to explore.

3. *Contract Negotiations*: Teachers and students should work together to negotiate a contract or agreement that includes the broad and specific topics (or an outline of the study), product ideas, materials required, time frames for milestones, and evaluation criteria (Riley, 2009). Teachers might also design or develop checklists or project planners to accompany the learning contract (Riley, 2009). Heacox (2002), Riley (2009), Smutny et al. (1997), and Winebrenner (2001) all created sample contracts. More information on contracts is also included later in this book.

4. *Working Conditions*: Winebrenner (2001) advocated for clear establishment of agreed-upon working conditions for students undertaking small-group or independent study projects. These are basically management goals, such as where study will take place (e.g., the classroom, a resource room, the library), how learning progress will be recorded (e.g., interviews, products), behavioral expectations (e.g., noise levels), where resources will be stored, and meeting deadlines and milestones. It is equally important that teachers establish their own working conditions, too: being available for regular progress checks and discussions, providing resources, and guaranteeing time within the daily and weekly schedules for students to work on their studies (Riley, 2009).

5. *Implementing the Study*: Johnsen and Goree (2009) explained that once a topic has been selected and the study organized, students are ready to begin asking complex questions that can be guided by the five Ws (who, what, where, when, why) and the H (how). Depending upon the questions being pursued, students then need to select an appropriate research or study method that extends beyond the library or the Internet. The selected method of inquiry should mirror those of the discipline(s) in which the topic sits. Collecting information

or data is the next task, and it can be helpful for students to analyze, synthesize, and evaluate their results with some teacher scaffolding. Students need to present their findings via a product, sharing what they have learned, and preferably via means that are of their own choice, appropriate for the intended audience, and multimodal.

6. *Evaluating the Study*: Finally, the study needs to be evaluated by the student, her peers, the audience, and/or the teacher. The content, processes, and product(s) of the study should be considered. In other words, it is important that student work is assessed based not just on outcomes, but also on the processes of investigation, asking questions like, "What would you do differently?" and, "Where could you go from here?"

As these guidelines indicate, there is a process for undertaking independent or small-group study that should be very clearly and explicitly taught to students. At each stage of enactment, teachers should facilitate student learning through clarity of goals, procedures, and expectations (Winebrenner, 2001). One way to prepare students for small-group or independent study is through using learning centers in the classroom (Heacox, 2002).

Learning Centers

There are many different types of learning centers described in the literature, but each provides opportunities for self-directed learning:

- A *challenge center* is an area in the classroom with a collection of activities and resources (Heacox, 2002). Tomlinson (1999) explained that these can be used for teaching, reinforcing, or extending a concept or skill from the curriculum.
- *Learning stations* also involve a wide range of activities and resources, but they require students to move simultaneously from task to task (Riley, 2009).

- *Browsing areas* are collections of resources focused on specific topics and may contain books, magazines, video and audio tapes, recommended websites, models, and other materials (Riley, 2009).
- *Learning spots* combine elements of the above approaches, and when used for gifted and talented students, they should provide depth and breadth on interesting and relevant topics, extending and moving beyond the regular curriculum at a speed or pace suitable to individual abilities (Riley, 2009).

Learning centers provide choice-driven opportunities for differentiated content, processes, and products (Riley, 2009), and they can be used with every age group and curriculum area (Heacox, 2002; Tomlinson, 1999). Learning centers can be part of everyday teacher planning as warm-up exercises or as cooldowns for early finishers, or they can be used on regular challenge days (Heacox, 2002). Themes or topics for centers can be based on the curriculum, but Tomlinson (1999) reported that there is greater motivational value in centers derived from students' interests. Other writers encourage the development of centers based on Howard Gardner's theory of multiple intelligences: logical-mathematical, visual-spatial, verbal-linguistic, musical, interpersonal and intrapersonal, naturalist, and bodily-kinesthetic areas in the classroom (Heacox, 2002; Riley, 2009; Smutny et al., 1997). A balance of purposes should drive the development of learning centers.

Developing learning centers is not dissimilar from other planning, and requires careful management to be successful. Once an area of focus has been chosen, teachers need to determine goals and objectives so they can design differentiated activities for meeting these. Because students undertake the activities independently or in small groups, and at their own pace, it is very important that directions are clear. There also needs to be a system for monitoring student involvement and evaluating performance. Finally, as with other provisions for gifted and talented students, it is important to determine the effectiveness of the center: what works, and what could be improved?

Learning centers need to entice students, inviting them to explore and engage in challenges, but they do not have to be elaborate! Centers should be eye-catching and attractive (Follis, 1993), located on bookshelves, in file folders, as display boards, in pocket charts, or as portable parcels (Riley, 2009). Coding by color, symbols, labels, or signs can help students make decisions about the level of work, the nature of the activity, or the pace of learning best suited to their strengths, interests, and needs. The key to making learning centers successful is the powerful combination of choice and independence, and this freedom can be granted through learning agreements between students and teachers.

Learning Agreements

As discussed in relation to independent or small-group study, learning agreements, or learning contracts, are good tools for managing self-directed study by balancing students' freedoms and choices with the teacher's expectations. Riley (2009) advocated that learning agreements should include the roles and responsibilities of the teacher. In other words, a learning agreement is not just student-focused and teacher-led, but "a more harmonious understanding or course of action" (Riley, 2009, p. 647). Depending on the purposes of the learning contract, parents, specialists, mentors, or other students might also become part of the negotiations and agreements. The collaborative writing of a learning agreement can be a stimulating experience for all parties, as it forces a constructive conversation about learning outcomes and how these will be achieved.

An agreement outlines the learning intentions, processes, time frames, resources, behaviors, outcomes, and expectations. Ways of working together, including working conditions (as explained previously), and consequences for failing to adhere to the agreed-upon terms are also included. A learning agreement can be enhanced by adding another layer of detailed implementation through personal agendas or lists of daily tasks (Tomlinson, 1999). As Riley (2009) explained, personal agendas are "planning guides facilitated by teachers with conferences and instructions and initialed by students and teachers as tasks are completed" (p. 647).

Learning agreements can range from closed-ended, teacher-driven, structured outlines of expectations to more open-ended, learner-driven "fill-in-the-blanks" (Riley, 2009). They lie on a continuum from fully self-directed to fully prescribed, and decisions regarding where to place an agreement on that scale depend upon students' and teachers' experiences, purposes, expectations, autonomy, and comfort zones. However, for gifted and talented students, motivation will increase with greater self-direction and independence (Riley, 2009), so it is best to steer away from teacher-driven agreements.

Here are some tips for the successful implementation of learning agreements:

- Remember, the emphasis is on the "learning," not the "agreement."
- Conduct a SWOT (Strengths, Weaknesses, Opportunities, and Threats) analysis with students. Focus on the strengths and weaknesses of their learning, the opportunities for learning, and the threats to learning.
- Ensure that the learning intentions are achievable and well matched to the time frames.
- Provide support for students in meeting their agreed-upon outcomes through time, resources, people, feedback and feed-forward, and encouragement.
- Encourage metacognitive thinking and analysis by asking students to reflect upon their learning experiences.
- Allow room for change and flexibility based on needs and progress.

Although learning agreements may sound like just another administrative tool (or more paperwork), they are based on the principles that teachers and students are partners in learning and that students are active, rather than merely passive or reactive, learners. Actively engaging gifted and talented students in their learning can also be facilitated by tiered instruction, as the next section describes.

Tiered Instruction

How do teachers ensure that all students, including gifted and talented students, learn a concept or skill to the best of their abilities, but also matched to their learning needs? One way to achieve this aim is through tiered instruction: layers of assignments, homework, tasks, strategies, or lessons matched to different levels of learning, readiness, or interests (Tomlinson, 1995). This approach builds upon prior knowledge by differentiating the complexity, depth, abstractness, and breadth through varying degrees of teacher direction, support, and input. Other factors to consider include the number of steps involved, the level of independence, and gauges of difficulty. When instruction is tiered, students work in different groups of varying size, learning the same concept but in different ways. The aim is to facilitate respectable work for all students.

The steps of tiered instruction, as outlined by Adams and Pierce (2006) are illustrated in Figure 2. Teachers begin by selecting a learning objective, goal, or standard. This is an important step and should not be confused by beginning with creating activities and then trying to mold them to fit! Next, teachers should determine what key concept or big idea all students should gain by asking themselves, "What do I want all students to learn at the end of this lesson?" At this stage, it is important to determine the background students bring to the concept and the foreground they need to be successful. In other words, what do students already know, and what do they need to know? Teachers then need to decide what to tier. Adams and Pierce (2006) recommended content, process, or product as frameworks for tiering. How will instruction be tiered—based on readiness, learning profile, or interest? The decisions made in these first five stages

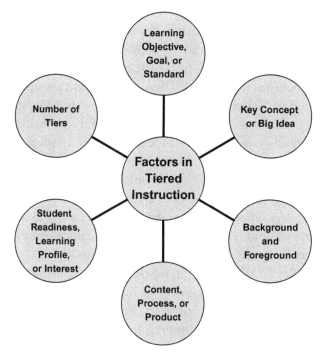

Figure 2. Factors in tiered instruction.

will determine the number of tiers. In some cases, the number of tiers will be dependent upon the range of ability levels. Adams (n.d.) recommended ability tiering as a means of meeting gifted and talented students' needs; when tiers are based on learning preferences or interests, all students are given choices, but at about the same level of difficulty. Example lessons can be found on the Ball State University Gifted and Talented Education page (http://gate.iweb.bsu.edu/Project_Gate).

Tiered instruction provides different pathways for students to learn the same key concepts (Adams, n.d.). It can be used in mixed-ability classrooms and also in programs for gifted and talented students. Implementing tiered instruction means grouping and regrouping students flexibly and in response to their needs.

Flexible Grouping

Flexible grouping, which has its roots in the traditional one-room schoolhouse, is not a new idea, but it has gained renewed interest with the recognition of the need to differentiate in today's inclusive classrooms. There are different grouping strategies used in classrooms; teachers can place students in ability groups, cooperative-learning groups, interests groups, student-led and teacher-led groups, student dyads, individual learning arrangements, and circles. Flexible grouping means that teachers formally and informally place students in a variety of ways. Groups may be teacher-selected, student-selected, ad hoc, or random, depending upon the planned objectives and activities, alongside student readiness, interests, and skills. Groups, therefore, may be heterogeneous or homogeneous.

As Riley (2009) stated, "in relation to regular classroom practices, students can and should be grouped for different purposes based on their strengths, interests, needs, and learning preferences" (p. 650). Flexible grouping acknowledges that all grouping patterns have value when they provide different experiences and different outcomes for students. It also requires teachers and students to be able to flow in and out of different working patterns throughout the day, within and across lessons. In other words, students are not in the same groups all of the time. Heacox (2002) outlined the hallmarks of flexible grouping as responsive and fluid, with different activities for different students.

Flexible grouping of gifted and talented students is not in conflict with inclusive education philosophies that call for heterogeneity (Tomlinson, 1999; Winebrenner, 2001). This is because the gifted and talented are not a homogeneous group, but rather a group of individuals with a wide range of abilities, skills, interests, strengths, and weaknesses. Flexible grouping means that gifted and talented students are not always in the same group with the same peers—no one is! As with the other strategies described in this book, flexible grouping is geared toward improving learning.

Meaningful Menus

Another tool for promoting learning is using planned opportunities for students to make choices from a range of possible activities targeted at simultaneously meeting the learning goals and the needs of students (Heacox, 2002; Smutny et al., 1997; Tomlinson, 1995; Winebrenner, 2001). A menu is a differentiation tool that offers students a collection of activities or tasks with which to demonstrate their learning. Normally, the learning activities will revolve around a specific concept or content area, with differentiated processes and products (Riley, 2009). Activities can be constructed based upon:

- ability or readiness levels (Tomlinson, 1999);
- complexity (Heacox, 2002);
- related topics (Winebrenner, 2001);
- cognitive progressions using Bloom's taxonomy (Riley, 2009; Winebrenner, 2001); or
- learning preferences or styles (Riley, 2009).

Meaningful menus also provide an opportunity for students to create their own options. The key to menus is the provision of choice—meaningful choice. Choice is an important way to motivate and interest gifted and talented students (Heacox, 2002).

There are many creative ways teachers can present students with choices, as Table 2 indicates. Teachers can use this tic-tac-toe board of nine options to select the ones best suited to their classrooms. Deciding which meaningful menu to use should be driven by how much time exists for development and completion of activities, as well as by the learning objectives matched to individual differences. "Teachers will no doubt have other ideas for creative ways of presenting students with options, but the bottom line when using menus . . . should always be to find more than one way of getting to the same destination" (Riley, 2009, p. 649).

Table 2
Meaningful Menu Tic-Tac-Toe

Choice Boards	Tic-Tac-Toe Menu	List Menu
Laminated cards placed in pockets on a bulletin board or wall hanging. Cards could also be in a card file. Another option is to use a computer file for cards.	Nine choices, with vertical, horizontal, and diagonal options for completion. The middle square is often a "free choice."	Choices are given point values, and students may choose any combination for a total score of 100. These choices are simply listed on paper.
Baseball Game	**Teacher's Choice!**	**2-5-8 Menu**
Completed choices of up to 100 runs: Singles are worth 10, doubles are 20, triples are 30, and homeruns are 100. Run values are increasingly difficult and challenging!	You might have other strategies for creating meaningful menus. Be creative and try your own ideas!	Choices are worth 2, 5, or 8 points, with increasing difficulty for increasing point value. Activities chosen must add up to 10 points. Try other numerical patterns, too!
Restaurant Menu	**Agendas**	**Multiple Intelligences Menu**
Choices include appetizers, entrees, and desserts, with different ingredients of complexity and different selections of activities.	Choices include imperatives, negotiables, and options for student selection. Agendas work well for older students, as they require some negotiation.	Choices are based on intelligences—either one intelligence or a range for selection. Similarly, Bloom's taxonomy can be used for menu choices.

Pulling It All Together in Your Own Classroom

These are just some of the recommended strategies for differentiation of content, processes, and products for gifted and talented students in inclusive classrooms. Teachers will find other ideas in the recommended resources at the end of this book, and of course, teachers have their own bags of tricks based on professional and personal experiences in the classroom coupled with professional learning and study. A differentiated learning environment for all students needs to be flexible, filled with choices and variety, and reflective of individual student differences identified and responded to by caring, creative teachers. For gifted and talented students, challenge based on complexity, abstractedness, depth, and breadth should be evidenced. No single strategy or practice will work; rather, a myriad of combinations is needed. Creating inclusive classrooms that meet the needs of gifted and talented students can be enhanced with schoolwide strategies and practices.

In Your School

Within schools, there is a need for overall coordination if teachers are to provide differentiated learning for gifted and talented students in general classrooms. Schoolwide approaches need to address professional learning and support, administrative leadership, and curricular structures and implementation (Riley, 2009). For example, to work effectively with gifted and talented learners, classroom teachers will need:

- advanced subject knowledge in order to provide content differentiation;
- deep curricular knowledge to make appropriate modifications;
- classroom management skills;
- pedagogical skills, including the tools of differentiation;
- resources that are accessible, appropriate, user-friendly, and supported with information on usage; and

- time for planning and collaboration (VanTassel-Baska & Stambaugh, 2005).

Some teachers may also need to have their beliefs and attitudes about gifted and talented students—and about their own roles as facilitators—challenged, reframed, and reshaped.

All teachers, therefore, need opportunities at pre- and in-service levels that will assist them in understanding and identifying the needs of gifted and talented students, qualitatively differentiating the curriculum using classroom-based strategies, and evaluating the effectiveness of practice (Riley, 2009). University educators, school leaders, and specialists in gifted and talented education need to take leading roles in ensuring that *all* classroom teachers at *all* levels have knowledge and skills in this area.

Overall school coordination of regular classroom services for gifted and talented students can be supported by curricular and administrative structures. Curriculum is defined most simply as, "a set of planned experiences for a targeted population" (VanTassel-Baska, 1994, p. xvi). It is a coherent structure with defined goals and purposes, attainable outcomes, and a prescribed time frame for learning (VanTassel-Baska, 1992). In addition to being coherent in nature, a curriculum should be comprehensive. These two components, coherence and comprehensiveness, are achieved through the development of a scope and sequence. Additionally, to meet the curriculum goals and objectives, units of instruction—or delivery ways and means—should be developed. As VanTassel-Baska (2000) stated, "Curriculum experiences for gifted learners need to be carefully planned, written down, and implemented in order to maximize their potential effect" (p. 345).

If curriculum experiences are not carefully planned and assessed, the risk is run of providing indefensible, unsustainable, inappropriate education for gifted and talented students. As Thompson (2000) stated, curriculum then becomes "an evolving process in the context of the classroom"; however, by considering the more serious side of curriculum, educators begin to live out the differences between "planning it and winging it . . . being careful and careless" (p. 1). Thus, not surprisingly, one recommended strategy for schoolwide differentiation is the adaptation or adoption of a curricular framework (Riley, 2009).

There are several curricular models for schoolwide improvement in gifted and talented education that can be implemented: the Schoolwide Enrichment Model (Renzulli & Reis, 1985); the Parallel Curriculum Model (Tomlinson et al., 2006a, 2006b); the Multiple Menu Model (Renzulli, Leppien, & Hays, 2000); the Integrated Curriculum Model (VanTassel-Baska, 1997); and the Pyryt Enrichment Matrix, or Pyryt's Ps (Pyryt & Bosetti, 2006). Each of these models provides a framework for providing differentiation in relation to content, process, and product modifications, and equally importantly, each does this from a strong theoretical and research base.

Pyryt's model (Pyryt & Bosetti, 2006) nicely summed up the key components of his ideas, which mirror those of other models, with his Five Ps for curriculum for gifted and talented learners:

1. *pace*: accelerated pace to address students' rapid rates of learning;
2. *process*: higher order and creative thinking to meet students' capacity for complex thought;
3. *passion*: inquiry that engages students in their areas of interest;
4. *product*: recognition of varied representations of knowledge, understandings, and skills; and
5. *peers*: opportunities for acceptance, including the chance for students to develop relationships with like-minded peers.

Kanevsky and Keighley (2003) created a similar set of key factors that can be seen in these curriculum models called the Five Cs: challenge, complexity, control, choice, and caring teachers. When exploring curriculum models, all of the ABCs of differentiation can be evidenced to varying extents, and so an eclectic approach can be taken—mixing and matching what best suits the needs of learners. More information about each of these can be found in the resource section at the end of this book.

Administratively, there are some other approaches that can be implemented in schools to ensure differentiation across all classrooms:

- *Enrichment clusters* are weekly 90-minute blocks of time for groups of students who share common interests, but who are not necessarily the same age or in the same grade, to work together with a facilitator to create a product, service, or performance (Renzulli, Gentry, & Reis, 2003).

- *Cluster grouping* places the top five to eight academically gifted students at one grade level in a classroom together with a teacher suited to meet their needs (Rogers, 2002). The remainder of the class is of mixed ability, but this creates a "mass" of like-minded peers in an inclusive classroom.

- *Cross-grade/age grouping or multiage classrooms* means that students are grouped into classrooms not strictly by age, but by their abilities in specific subjects (Riley, 2009; Rogers, 2002).

- *Looping* places teachers with the same students for 2 or more years (Grant, 1997; Tomlinson & Allan, 2000). This strategy enables teachers and students to develop long-term partnerships in learning.

- *Mentorships* can be explored for individual students or groups of students, easing the potential burden of differentiation for regular classroom teachers with an injection of external expertise and passion for gifted and talented students (Heacox, 2002; Riley, 2009).

- *Weekly planning* uses a team approach, can incorporate short- and long-term differentiated goals, and can be supported by using frameworks like Bloom's taxonomy or Gardner's multiple intelligences in isolation or in tandem (Heacox, 2002; Smutny et al., 1997). Heacox's (2002) Content Catalysts, Processes, and Product

(CCPP) Toolkit is another easy tool for planning learning experiences.

Providing structure and support on a schoolwide basis will better ensure differentiated learning for gifted and talented students in inclusive classrooms. But how do teachers know if their efforts are paying off? Ways to check for differentiation are explored in the following chapter.

Checking for Differentiation in Inclusive Classrooms

The strategies recommended in this book appear to be sound, and they are certainly gaining momentum and attention by many teachers in classrooms. However, although there is a growing body of empirical research exploring the implementation, maintenance, and impact of differentiated learning in all classrooms, it remains rather limited (Riley, 2009). Despite greater efforts in professional development and collaboration among specialists and regular classroom teachers, there are few studies available to indicate or support differentiation in all classrooms (VanTassel-Baska & Stambaugh, 2005). In an era when evidence-based teaching is desirable, without this research, teachers must actively engage in their own evaluation and reflection, gathering data to support what works and what does not work for gifted and talented students.

One way to do this is to check for differentiation by using evaluation scales. The Classroom Observation Scale (VanTassel-Baska & Feng, 2007) and The Differentiated Classroom Observation Scale (Cassady et al., 2004) are two tools that can be used by external observers, such as colleagues, gifted and talented specialists, or school principals. These scales can also be used by teachers who might videotape their lessons for later viewing, or as guidelines for active, structured, critical reflection. Teachers can also use action research, or what Eyre (2006) called "structured tinkering." Using action research, teachers can move through cycles of reflection that lead to the development of understanding and the testing of interventions. Riley and Moltzen (2010) recommended action research as a model for evaluation that offers flexibility and fluidity—two elements especially needed in the parallel evolution of innovative teaching and testing for effectiveness. Regardless of the approach or approaches taken, it is important that teachers test the effectiveness of differentiated learning for gifted and talented students in inclusive classrooms.

Conclusion

A group of gifted and talented secondary students, when asked to provide advice for preservice teachers, said to tell them, "If you want to do it, you will do it!" Teachers wanting to make a difference for their gifted and talented students in today's diverse classrooms can implement, maintain, and evaluate a range of qualitatively differentiated strategies—as individuals and as a team. Gifted and talented students need to have their unique abilities and qualities recognized, accepted, affirmed, and encouraged. Teachers in inclusive classrooms will provide the catalysts for their individuality to be celebrated—then the gifted and talented, too, will feel a sense of belonging in today's diverse communities of learners.

Recommended Reading: Books

Adams, C. M., & Pierce, R. L. (2006). *Differentiating instruction: A practical guide for tiering lessons in the elementary grades.* Waco, TX: Prufrock Press.

This practical guide provides elementary classroom teachers with a step-by-step approach to implementing tiered lessons for all learners. It includes advice on grouping students by ability, interests, and learning styles, as well as a template for creating tiered lessons.

Heacox, D. (2002). *Differentiating instruction in the regular classroom: How to reach and teach all learners, grades 3–12.* Minneapolis, MN: Free Spirit.

This book is designed for teachers of all learners in grades 3–12 who want to meet the needs of their students in differentiated classrooms. The resource begins by explaining differentiation in principle, and then moves teachers into exploring differentiation in action. It includes many practical, reproducible aids for teachers and their students.

Karnes, F. A., & Bean, S. M. (2009). *Methods and materials for teaching gifted and talented students* (3rd ed.). Waco, TX: Prufrock Press.

This textbook is a comprehensive guide to understanding the methods and materials for teaching gifted and talented students of all ages and in all settings. Written by experts in gifted education, it provides sound ideas for practice grounded in current theory and research.

Renzulli, J. S. (1994). *Schools for talent development: A practical plan for total school improvement.* Mansfield Center, CT: Creative Learning Press.

This book aims to provide a practical plan for schoolwide improvement based on the Schoolwide Enrichment Model. This model provides for a continuum of approaches, including identification of gifted behaviors using multiple methods and provisions in the regular classroom and beyond.

Renzulli, J. S., Gentry, M., & Reis, S. M. (2003). *Enrichment clusters: A practical plan for real-world, student-driven learning.* Mansfield Center, CT: Creative Learning Press.

This guide provides schools with ideas and advice for developing schoolwide enrichment clusters for all students and teachers. Although these clusters operate outside of the regular classroom, they can complement the curriculum, and the methods provided by the authors for identifying students' strengths and interests are relevant to all teachers.

Renzulli, J. S., Leppien, J. H., & Hays, T. S. (2000). *The Multiple Menu Model: A practical guide for developing differentiated curriculum.* Mansfield Center, CT: Creative Learning Press.

This curriculum model can be used by all teachers to plan challenging, relevant, and meaningful learning experiences in their classrooms. The guidebook provides teachers with a deeper understanding of a discipline, its content and skills, and methodologies and techniques for teaching.

Renzulli, J. S., & Reis, S. M. (1985). *The Schoolwide Enrichment Model: A comprehensive plan for educational excellence*. Mansfield Center, CT: Creative Learning Press.

Schools wanting to address gifted and talented students in all classrooms, across a continuum of approaches, will want to adopt this comprehensive model. Classroom teachers will find the curricular guidance and practical, reproducible resources invaluable for differentiating in their classrooms.

Roberts, J. L., & Inman, T. F. (2009). *Strategies for differentiating instruction: Best practices for the classroom* (2nd ed.). Waco, TX: Prufrock Press.

This is an easy-to-use book that provides classroom teachers with techniques and strategies for ensuring that students are challenged and demonstrate continuous progress in their learning. This book is designed for novices in differentiating instruction, providing a good starting point.

Smutny, J. F., Walker, S. Y., & Meckstroth, E. A. (1997). *Teaching young gifted children in the regular classroom: Identifying, nurturing, and challenging ages 4–9*. Minneapolis, MN: Free Spirit.

Teachers of young gifted children (ages 4–9) will benefit from this book, which provides practical advice on differentiating in all classrooms. Teachers are provided with invaluable information on identification of strengths and abilities, which then triggers a raft of ideas for providing challenge to young gifted learners.

Tomlinson, C. A. (1999). *The differentiated classroom: Responding to the needs of all learners*. Alexandria, VA: Association for Supervision and Curriculum Development.

This book is perhaps the classic guide to differentiation in all classrooms, for all learners. The book provides teachers with theoretical and practical suggestions, including lessons for both elementary and secondary levels across several curriculum areas.

Tomlinson, C. A. (2001). *How to differentiate instruction in mixed-ability classrooms* (2nd ed.). Alexandria, VA: Association for Supervision and Curriculum Development.

Students in mixed-ability classrooms may need scaffolds or high-speed elevators to succeed in having their needs met, and this book shows teachers how to differentiate content, processes, and products in their planning across the curriculum.

Tomlinson, C. A., Kaplan, S. N., Renzulli, J. S., Purcell, J., Leppien, J., & Burns, D. (2002). *The parallel curriculum: A design to develop potential and challenge high-ability learners.* Thousand Oaks, CA: Corwin Press.

This curriculum model provides challenging learning opportunities for all students through four rich parallels, with ascending intellectual demands suitable for gifted learners. Schools and individual teachers wanting guidance on creating challenging curriculum for gifted students in their classrooms while still meeting the basic level of skill and understanding some students require will enjoy this model.

Winebrenner, S. (2001). *Teaching gifted kids in the regular classroom: Strategies and techniques every teacher can use to meet the academic needs of the gifted and talented* (Rev. ed.). Minneapolis, MN: Free Spirit.

This book is a must-have for every elementary and middle school classroom teacher. It provides an array of practical strategies teachers can use daily, and these strategies are supplemented by reproducible forms, planners, and guides (included on a CD). Although many strategies will be appropriate for the range of students in inclusive classrooms, these are specifically recommended and appropriate for gifted learners.

Recommended Reading: Articles

Brimijoin, K., Marquisee, E., & Tomlinson, C. (2003). Using data to differentiate instruction. *Educational Leadership, 60*(5), 70–72.

This article offers an overview of how one teacher used assessment data to differentiate instruction.

Moon, T. R. (2005). The role of assessment in differentiation. *Theory Into Practice, 44,* 226–233.

Moon explores the vital role that assessment plays in the success of a differentiated classroom. The emphasis is on educators using the results from assessments to inform the instructional sequence, thereby providing all learners the support and opportunities needed for success.

Ozturk, M. A., & Debelak, C. (2008). Academic competitions as tools for differentiation in middle school. *Gifted Child Today, 31*(3), 47–53.

Academic competitions can be effective tools for differentiation even when school resources to support differentiated instruction are limited. Differentiation of content, process, product, and learning environment are all discussed within the context of academic competitions.

Powers, E. (2008). The use of independent study as a viable differentiation technique for gifted learners in the regular classroom. *Gifted Child Today, 31*(3), 57–65.

Here, independent study is examined as a viable differentiation tool for gifted learners in the regular classroom. Using data obtained from 16 gifted seventh-grade social studies students and three teachers, the author presents results on student choice, the use of independent study, and the link between social studies and real-world experiences as motivating factors for student achievement.

Tomlinson, C. (2000). Reconcilable differences: Standards-based teaching and differentiation. *Educational Leadership, 58*(1), 6–11.

Standards-based teaching and differentiated learning can be combined in the classroom. The characteristics of both differentiation and standards-based teaching are outlined, and negative and positive examples of using both approaches together are presented.

Websites

Carol Ann Tomlinson

http://www.caroltomlinson.com

Best known for her work with differentiated instruction, Carol Tomlinson created a website that is a great starting point for those trying to locate books, articles, and other resources pertaining to differentiation.

Differentiation Central

http://differentiationcentral.com

A service of the Institutes on Academic Diversity at the University of Virginia's Curry School of Education, this site provides a place for teachers to share lesson plans, strategies, and other resources on differentiation. Visitors to this site also have access to planning templates, informative videos, and podcasts to support differentiation in the classroom.

DVDs

Association for Supervision and Curriculum Development. (Producer). (2005). *The common sense of differentiation: Meeting specific learner needs in the regular classroom* [DVD]. Available from http://shop.ascd.org/VIDEOS.aspx

This series of six workshops was designed for use by classroom teachers, teaching specialists, curriculum developers, curriculum coordinators, and others interested in designing classrooms that maximize the potential of a full range of learners.

Association for Supervision and Curriculum Development. (Producer). (2008). *Differentiated instruction in action* [DVD]. Available from http://shop.ascd.org/VIDEOS.aspx

Carol Ann Tomlinson and classroom teachers bring differentiated instruction to life in this practical, easily implemented professional development program available for the elementary, middle, and high school levels.

Law, K., Forman, K. W., & Bureau of Education & Research. (Producers). (2009). *Using practical differentiation strategies to meet the learning needs of gifted students, grades 2–6* [DVD]. Available from http://www.berproducts.org/video-training. html

Classroom teachers demonstrate successful strategies for differentiating lessons and activities for their gifted students. Strategies shown include tiered assignments, flexible grouping, providing choices, orbital studies, and curriculum buyouts.

References

Adams, C. M. (n.d.). *Critical questions about tiered lessons.* Retrieved from http://gate.iweb.bsu.edu/Project_Gate/Instruction/criticalquestions.htm

Adams, C. M., & Pierce, R. L. (2006). *Differentiating instruction: A practical guide for tiering lessons in the elementary grades.* Waco, TX: Prufrock Press.

Betts, G. (2004). Fostering autonomous learners through levels of differentiation. *Roeper Review, 26,* 190–191.

Braggett, E. J. (1994). *Developing programs for gifted students: A total school approach.* Victoria, Australia: Hawker Brownlow.

Brighton, C. M. (2005). Preassessment: A differentiation power tool. *Teaching for High Potential, 1*(1), 2–5.

Cassady, J. C., Speirs Neumeister, K. L., Adams, C. M., Cross, T. L., Dixon, F. A., & Pierce, R. L. (2004). The Differentiated Classroom Observation Scale. *Roeper Review, 26,* 139–146.

Douglas, D. (2004, December). Four simple steps to self-advocacy. *Parenting for High Potential.* Retrieved from http://www.davidsongifted.org/db/Articles_id_10458.aspx

Eyre, D. (2006). Structured tinkering: Improving provisions for the gifted in ordinary schools. In C. M. M. Smith (Ed.), *Including the gifted and talented: Making inclusion work for more gifted and able learners* (pp. 161–175). New York, NY: Routledge.

Follis, H. D. (1993). A step-by-step plan for developing learning centers. In C. J. Maker (Ed.), *Critical issues in gifted education: Programs for the gifted in regular classrooms* (pp. 296–304). Austin, TX: PRO-ED.

George, D. (1997). *The challenge of the able child* (2nd ed.). London, UK: Fulton.

Grant, J. (1997). *Looping Q & A.* Peterborough, NH: Crystal Springs Books.

Heacox, D. (2002). *Differentiating instruction in the regular classroom: How to reach and teach all learners, grades 3–12.* Minneapolis, MN: Free Spirit.

Johnsen, S. (2005). Guiding without taking over: A parent's role in independent study. *The Duke Gifted Letter, 5*(3). Retrieved from http://www.dukegiftedletter.com/articles/vol5no3_connex.html

Johnsen, S. K., & Goree, K. (2005). *Independent study for gifted learners.* Waco, TX: Prufrock Press.

Johnsen, S. K., & Goree, K. K. (2009). Teaching gifted students through independent study. In F. A. Karnes & S. M. Bean (Eds.), *Methods and materials for teaching the gifted* (3rd ed., pp. 415–446). Waco, TX: Prufock Press.

Kanevsky, L., & Keighley, T. (2003). To produce or not to produce? Understanding boredom and the honor in underachievement. *Roeper Review, 26,* 20–28.

Kettle, K. E., Renzulli, J. S., & Rizza, M. G. (n.d.). *Exploring student preferences for product development: My Way . . . An Expression Style Instrument.* Retrieved from http://www.gifted.uconn.edu/sem/exprstyl.html

Kincher, J. (1995). *Psychology for kids: 40 fun experiments that help you learn about yourself.* Minneapolis, MN: Free Spirit.

McGrail, L. (2005). *Modifying regular classroom curriculum for gifted and talented students.* Retrieved from http://www.prufrock.com/client/client_pages/Modfying_Curriculum.cfm

McIntyre, T., & Mery, W. (2004). *Parents' unofficial guide to gifted IEPs and gifted IEP meetings*. Retrieved from http://www.hoagiesgifted.org/unofficial_guide.htm

Pyryt, M. C., & Bosetti, B. L. (2006). Accommodating gifted learners in regular classrooms: Promises and pitfalls. In C. M. M. Smith (Ed.), *Including the gifted and talented: Making inclusion work for more gifted and able learners* (pp. 141–160). New York, NY: Routledge.

Reis, S. M., Burns, D. E., & Renzulli, J. S. (1992). *Curriculum compacting: The complete guide to modifying the regular curriculum for high-ability students*. Mansfield Center, CT: Creative Learning Press.

Renzulli, J. S. (1996). *The Interest-A-Lyzer family of instruments: A manual for teachers*. Mansfield Center, CT: Creative Learning Press.

Renzulli, J. S., Gentry, M., & Reis, S. M. (2003). *Enrichment clusters: A practical plan for real-world, student-driven learning*. Mansfield Center, CT: Creative Learning Press.

Renzulli, J. S., Leppien, J. H., & Hays, T. S. (2000). *The Multiple Menu Model: A practical guide for developing differentiated curriculum*. Mansfield Center, CT: Creative Learning Press.

Renzulli, J. S., & Reis, S. M. (1985). *The Schoolwide Enrichment Model: A comprehensive plan for educational excellence*. Mansfield Center, CT: Creative Learning Press.

Renzulli, J. S., & Reis, S. M. (n.d.). *Research related to the Schoolwide Enrichment Model*. Retrieved from http://www.sp.uconn.edu/~nrcgt/sem/rrsem.html

Riley, T., & Moltzen, R. (2010). *Enhancing and igniting talent development initiatives: Research to determine effectiveness*. Wellington, New Zealand: Ministry of Education.

Riley, T. L. (2009). Teaching gifted and talented students in regular classrooms. In F. A. Karnes & S. M. Bean (Eds.), *Methods and materials for teaching the gifted* (3rd ed., pp. 631–672). Waco, TX: Prufock Press.

Roberts, J. L., & Roberts, R. A. (2009). Writing units that remove the learning ceiling. In F. A. Karnes & S. M. Bean (Eds.),

Methods and materials for teaching the gifted (3rd ed., pp. 187–220). Waco, TX: Prufock Press.

Rogers, K. B. (2002). *Re-forming gifted education: How parents and teachers can match the program to the child.* Dayton, OH: Great Potential Press.

Siegle, D. (1998, Spring). An independent study model for secondary students. *NRC/GT Newsletter.* Retrieved from http://www.gifted.uconn.edu/nrcgt/newsletter/spring98/sprng987.html

Smutny, J. F., Walker, S. Y., & Meckstroth, E. A. (1997). *Teaching young gifted children in the regular classroom: Identifying, nurturing, and challenging ages 4–9.* Minneapolis, MN: Free Spirit.

Thompson, M. C. (2000, March). *Curriculum as profound engagement with the world.* Keynote address at the National Curriculum Networking Conference, The College of William and Mary. Retrieved from http://cfge.wm.edu/Gifted%20Educ%20Artices/CurriculumProfound.htm

Tomlinson, C. A. (1995). *How to differentiate instruction in mixed-ability classrooms.* Alexandria, VA: Association for Supervision and Curriculum Development.

Tomlinson, C. A. (1999). *The differentiated classroom: Responding to the needs of all learners.* Alexandria, VA: Association for Supervision and Curriculum Development.

Tomlinson, C. A. (2004). Sharing responsibility for differentiating instruction. *Roeper Review, 26,* 188–189.

Tomlinson, C. A., & Allan, S. D. (2000). *Leadership for differentiating schools and classrooms.* Alexandria, VA: Association for Supervision and Curriculum Development.

Tomlinson, C. A., Kaplan, S. N., Purcell, J. H., Leppien, J. H., Burns, D. E., & Strickland, C. A. (2006a). *The parallel curriculum in the classroom: Book 1.* Thousand Oaks, CA: Corwin Press.

Tomlinson, C. A., Kaplan, S. N., Purcell, J. H., Leppien, J. H., Burns, D. E., & Strickland, C. A. (2006b). *The parallel curriculum in the classroom: Book 2.* Thousand Oaks, CA: Corwin Press.

VanTassel-Baska, J. (1992). *Developing learner outcomes for gifted students* (ERIC Digest #E514). Reston, VA: Clearinghouse on Disabilities and Gifted Education.

VanTassel-Baska, J. (Ed.). (1994). *Comprehensive curriculum for gifted learners* (2nd ed.). Boston, MA: Allyn & Bacon.

VanTassel-Baska, J. (1997). What matters in curriculum for gifted learners: Reflections on theory, research, and practice. In N. Colangelo & G. A. Davis (Eds.), *Handbook of gifted education* (2nd ed., pp. 126–135). Needham Heights, MA: Allyn & Bacon.

VanTassel-Baska, J. (2000). Theory and research on curriculum development for the gifted. In K. A. Heller, F. J. Mönks, R. J. Sternberg, & R. F. Subotnik (Eds.), *The international handbook of giftedness and talent* (2nd ed., pp. 345–366). Oxford, UK: Elsevier Science.

VanTassel-Baska, J., & Feng, A. (2007). The development and use of a structured teacher observation scale to assess differentiated best practice. *Roeper Review, 19,* 89–92.

VanTassel-Baska, J., & Stambaugh, T. (2005). Challenges and possibilities for serving gifted learners in the regular classroom. *Theory Into Practice, 44,* 211–217.

Winebrenner, S. (2001). *Teaching gifted kids in the regular classroom: Strategies and techniques every teacher can use to meet the academic needs of the gifted and talented* (Rev. ed.). Minneapolis, MN: Free Spirit.

Associate Professor Tracy Riley, Ph.D., specializes in gifted and talented education. She teaches undergraduate and postgraduate courses in the field in addition to supervising postgraduate research. Tracy is the coeditor of *APEX: The New Zealand Journal of Gifted Education* and is on the editorial board of *Gifted Child Today*. An active advocate for gifted and talented students, Tracy has served on numerous Ministry of Education advisory groups and has coauthored the Ministry handbook, *Gifted and Talented Students: Meeting Their Needs in New Zealand Schools*. She publishes and presents widely at both national and international levels. In 2007, Tracy was awarded the Vice-Chancellor's Award for Sustained Excellence in Teaching and was the recipient of a national Tertiary Teaching Excellence Award. Tracy is a member of the executive committee of the Ako Aoteoroa Academy of Tertiary Teaching Excellence and is chairperson of the board for giftEDnz, The Professional Association for Gifted Education.

Printed in the United States
by Baker & Taylor Publisher Services